LITTL[E]
CRIMINOLOGY

Rasha Barrage

THE LITTLE BOOK OF CRIMINOLOGY

An Hachette UK Company
www.hachette.co.uk

Summersdale Publishers
Part of Octopus Publishing Group Limited
Carmelite House
50 Victoria Embankment
LONDON
EC4Y 0DZ
UK

www.summersdale.com

Printed and bound in Poland

ISBN: 978-1-83799-302-4

Substantial discounts on bulk quantities of Summersdale books are available to corporations, professional associations and other organizations. For details contact general enquiries: telephone: +44 (0) 1243 771107 or email: enquiries@summersdale.com.

Contents

Introduction

"Death and taxes" are often cited as the only two certainties in life. However, there is a third element: crime. Since laws were created, there has always been a minority of individuals who try to break them. One of the oldest written laws, the Code of Hammurabi, composed in 1750 BCE, included brutal punishments "to make justice visible in the land, to destroy the wicked person and the evildoer". Nearly 4,000 years later, the shadowy realms of criminal networks and transnational misdeeds are expanding at an unprecedented rate. Our dynamic society breeds a whole spectrum of wrongdoing, from petty theft to cybercrime.

This book introduces you to the world of criminology and reveals why crimes *are* preventable and offenders are not simply "evil". You will explore big questions in the discipline, such as: What causes someone to offend? Why do crime rates vary in different areas? By exploring crime from a variety of angles, you will see how criminology plays a big part in managing deviance and designing safer societies.

WHAT IS
CRIMINOLOGY?

The term "criminology" is a combination of the Latin *crimen*, meaning accusation, and the Greek *logiā*, meaning the study of. Today, criminology is known as the scientific study of crime. As one of the largest and fastest growing branches of sociology, it explores crime as a social rather than a legal phenomenon. Lawyers are concerned with the content of the law, the legal process and if an individual has committed a specific offence. In contrast, criminologists investigate why people engage in illegal behaviour when actions are outlawed and how to prevent offending generally.

This chapter sets out the meaning of crime and introduces you to the science and research that defines criminology. The different elements of a crime will be explained, such as intent and harm, to show how the different parts shape criminological theories. The presentation of crime in the media will also be discussed, and how it can influence the criminal justice system. With a clearer understanding of the discipline, you will see how criminologists play a central part in challenging and disrupting society's approach to crime.

Crime

An intentional act or omission in violation of criminal law… committed without defense or justification, and sanctioned by the state as a felony or misdemeanor.
Paul Tappan, American criminologist

In comparison with civil law, a crime is an act that violates criminal law, like murder or theft. Unlike torts, which are wrongful acts against private individuals (which can lead to civil action, such as negligence), crime relates to offences against the public or the state. This means that the classification of crimes and responses to them depend on the culture and political environment of each society.

These differences are all decided and enforced by people, and this is why criminology falls under the umbrella discipline of sociology, which is the organized study of human societies, their interactions, and the causes and consequences of human behaviour. Criminologists look beyond the strict legal definition of crime and examine the social and cultural roots of crime and criminalization, as well as how states respond to deviant behaviour.

Deviance

Criminological research goes beyond crime and explores all actions that wander from the norm. Some studies focus on rebellious behaviour or "deviants" – those who break social rules or group expectations. Deviance can be criminal or non-criminal, and its definition varies across cultures. **Formal deviant behaviour** refers to actions that violate formal laws, while **informal deviant behaviour** refers to actions that violate social norms. All forms of deviance can result in negative consequences. For example, if you break the law, you could be fined or arrested, and if you break social etiquette, you may be ostracized by your peers. Studying deviance helps criminologists understand how **social control** operates and the way cultural norms shape individual behaviour.

NORMS

Social norms are unwritten rules that guide your conduct in society (such as not standing too close to strangers). Normative crimes are acts that offend a moral code of behaviour, like keeping cash found in the street or playing loud music at night.

Measuring crime

Crime and deviance can be measured by a range of methods, including:

Official crime statistics – data from law enforcement agencies, such as the police. This can show the types of crimes being committed, the demographics of offenders and the geographic distribution of crime. These statistics are influenced by police practices, reporting biases and victims' willingness to report crimes.

Surveys and interviews with the public – surveys gather public information, and interviews provide individual in-depth reaction. Both methods give valuable insights into people's experiences with crime, plus their beliefs and attitudes towards crime and deviance.

Observational studies – watching and recording criminal or deviant activity in natural settings (e.g. the street or public places) or analyzing behaviour through controlled experiments. This can reveal environmental factors leading to crime.

Case studies – in-depth examination of a single case or small number of cases. This can show the background and motivation of offenders.

A rendezvous discipline

Criminologists ask a wide range of questions to develop theories and strategies to address crime. For example:

- **Nature and extent** – what types of crimes are being committed and where?

- **Causes** – how do social inequality, individual psychology and economic factors contribute to crime?

- **Consequences** – how does the criminal justice system treat offenders and victims? How do policies affect offenders and victims?

- **Reactions** – how are offenders with different characteristics and circumstances handled within the system? What forms of punishment exist, and how effective are they?

- **Prevention** – what preventive measures can be implemented to reduce crime?

Answering these questions requires insights from psychology, economics, philosophy and even biology. The central theme of human wrongdoing is explored through multidisciplinary perspectives, which is why criminology is sometimes described as a "rendezvous discipline": the point where different disciplines meet.

Seeing the big picture

Criminologists try to gain a holistic understanding of crime by incorporating knowledge from different fields. For instance:

- Anthropology shows how cultural values, rituals and socialization processes may shape attitudes towards crime.

- Biology shows that behaviour can be influenced by genetic predisposition, brain functioning and biological factors, such as traumatic brain injuries or the influence of hormones.

- Economics examines the role of poverty, unemployment and economic inequality in driving criminal activity.

- Psychology helps to understand individual motivations, cognitive processes and personality traits that may influence criminal behaviour.

- Philosophy explores ethical questions around punishment, justice and the moral implications of lawbreaking.

- Sociology provides insights into social structures, cultural norms and group dynamics that influence crime rates.

This interdisciplinary approach lets criminologists develop evidence-based policies to tackle crime and promote safer communities.

Elements of a crime

For criminal liability to be established, the following elements are usually considered:

CRIMINAL ACT

This is known as the *actus reus* or the (external) physical element of a crime. This covers the circumstances and the outcome of a person's conduct, such as pointing a gun at someone.

CRIMINAL INTENT

This is known as the *mens rea* or the (internal) mental element of a crime. It literally means having "a guilty mind" and refers to the intent and determination someone has when committing a crime. It is a lot harder to prove than the physical element.

CONCURRENCE

The *actus reus* and *mens rea* must occur at the same time. Therefore, a person is usually convicted of a crime when they have committed an offensive act – or omission – with intent to do so. This doesn't apply to "strict liability" crimes where intent is not necessary, like speeding or parking offences.

CAUSATION

There should be a causal link between the act and the result. In other words, the act (or crime) must be the direct cause of the harm.

HARM

The injury, damage or loss caused by the crime. This can be physical, emotional, financial or social in nature.

ATTENDANT CIRCUMSTANCE

The context in which the offence took place, including time, place, the criminal's prior knowledge of the details of the offence (such as knowing the victim or the value of an item they then intend to steal) and the relationship between parties.

The specific elements vary across different jurisdictions and depend on the offence being considered.

I SMELL A RAT!

In medieval Europe, it was believed that "crimes" committed by animals were the devil's work and letting them go unpunished would entice the devil to take over human affairs. From the thirteenth to eighteenth centuries, dogs, pigs, cows and rats were put on trial for offences like murder and criminal damage. Modern criminal justice systems recognize that animals lack the criminal intent to be accountable for their actions.

Media presentation

The media has a profound influence in shaping how we perceive crime. By selecting which crimes to highlight, which perpetrators to spotlight and which victims to empathize with, the media can craft a reality that may not align with the statistical truth. Vivid and compelling stories of isolated incidents of crime can sway the public to believe that they reflect a widespread trend and magnify the fear of crime. The criminologist Stanley Cohen developed the term "moral panics" to describe how exaggerated media coverage portrays certain groups as deviant and threatening to society, especially youth subcultures (see page 110).

Criminologists have explored how the media oversimplifies criminal behaviour and often highlights the psychological state of criminals rather than the wider social context. For instance, news coverage usually includes interviews with victims or police but no expert analysis about the possible causes. The media also concentrates on victims' emotions and harsh punishments instead of rehabilitation or alternative forms of justice, like restorative justice (see page 132).

Media influence

The relationship between media and crime is a continuous source of debate for criminologists. Interesting theories include:

HYPODERMIC SYRINGE MODEL

Also known as the "magic bullet" model, this theory argues that media messages (such as sexism and racism) are like a drug injected directly into the audience's mind, who then passively receive whatever they are told without question.

"COPYCAT" BEHAVIOUR

Individuals can be influenced to imitate criminal behaviour they see on screen, including fictional characters (see page 96).

DESENSITIZATION

A controversial issue is whether depictions of violence on screen encourage viewers to behave in a similar manner, especially children. The psychologist Elizabeth Newson argued that children's continuous exposure to aggression over several years desensitizes them to violence, so they see it as the norm or a solution to problems.

Researchers often emphasize that the media is just one of many influences that shape criminal behaviour.

Social media

Until the early part of the twenty-first century, individuals who committed crimes often did so secretly, away from the eyes of society and law enforcement. Since the advent of social media, it's increasingly common that offenders boast about their criminal behaviour to friends and followers online – a phenomenon known as **"performance crime"**. For instance, in the early 2020s, there was a notable increase in thefts of Hyundai and Kia cars. This surge was caused by the widespread sharing of videos that showed how to exploit security vulnerabilities in these vehicles.

While there have always been criminals seeking attention and recognition, social media allows crime footage to reach large audiences quickly. Social media has allowed new types of crime to develop, like "revenge porn", and it has given offenders more opportunities to identify targets. Terrorist organizations use social media for recruitment, propaganda and fund raising, sharing strategies for attacks and data mining. However, social media can be a helpful tool for police investigations as it provides unprecedented access to the public and real-time incidents.

A BRIEF HISTORY OF CRIMINOLOGY

The origins of criminology can be traced back to ancient civilizations when social rules were established to maintain order. For thousands of years, justice focused on retribution and punishment, often based on religious beliefs. Ancient Greece and Rome, for instance, had legal systems that emphasized punitive measures such as exile, or death by poisoning or crucifixion.

During the Middle Ages, the practice of "trial by ordeal" relied on divine intervention to determine guilt or innocence. By the eighteenth century, some prominent thinkers like Cesare Beccaria and Jeremy Bentham began to question the role of punishment and advocated for proportionate penalties. This chapter explores how early ideas paved the way for criminology to emerge as a distinct field in the nineteenth century. You will be introduced to pioneering figures and theories about the causes of crime and criminal behaviour. With an understanding of the origins and evolution of criminology, you will see how the forces of politics and society have influenced its development and will continue to do so.

Blood feuds

From ancient grudge break to new mutiny,
Where civil blood makes civil hands unclean.
William Shakespeare, *Romeo and Juliet*

Can you imagine a life without rules? Laws and rules are themselves a rule of life. This book is written according to certain rules of language. If you travelled outside today, you probably followed traffic laws. If you see someone being violent, you expect the person to be punished according to the law.

However, for centuries across the world people experienced a different life. Without formal legal systems and weak or absent law enforcement, individuals and families often took matters of justice into their own hands. Crimes led to the earliest form of punishment: **private revenge**. This often resulted in prolonged conflicts between families or clans. Eventually, pioneering thinkers realized that rules of crime and punishment needed to be established. These thinkers include Confucius and Athenian lawmaker Draco (whose punishments inspired the word "draconian"). They realized rules were needed to maintain order and prevent private retaliation.

An eye for an eye

The first theories of crime and punishment were based on ideas of retribution and deterrence. **Retribution** is the idea that punishment should be inflicted on the wrongdoer as a form of revenge or retaliation. As far back as 2000 BCE, civilizations including Mesopotamia and ancient Egypt believed that imposing suffering or harm on an offender, thereby taking revenge on wrongdoers, would restore balance and order in society. Punishments were designed to match the severity of crimes committed.

Supporters of the **deterrence** principle believed that harsh punishments, such as public humiliation, mutilation or death, would discourage others from committing similar crimes. The Law of the Twelve Tables in Rome, written around 450 BCE, aimed to intimidate criminals through the threat of severe consequences, such as flogging, being sold into slavery or death. The laws were inscribed on 12 bronze tablets and publicly displayed, making them accessible to all citizens.

Vice versus crime

During the thirteenth century, the Italian theologian Saint Thomas Aquinas argued that most people are weak and imperfect. Building on the ancient philosophies of Plato, Aristotle and Seneca, he distinguished between "vices" as immoral or potentially self-harming behaviour (like excessive drinking) and "crimes" as behaviour that harms others and the offender's essential "humanness" (like robbery or murder). Aquinas argued that laws should not punish vices but that punishments for crimes were required to maintain order and justice. He emphasized the value of mercy and rehabilitation to reform the offender and encourage their return to virtuous living.

COMPURGATION

Trial by ordeal became rarer during the thirteenth century and was replaced by **"compurgation"**, in which the accused gathered a group of 12 reputable people to swear their innocence. The idea was that no one would lie under oath for fear of being punished by God. Compurgation later evolved into testimony under oath and trial by jury.

Classical school

It is better to prevent crimes than to punish them.
Cesare Beccaria

In 1764, an obscure Italian lawyer named Cesare Beccaria published a book that became one of the most influential legal essays of all time. Titled *Dei delitti e delle pene* (*On Crimes and Punishments*), it was the first succinct and organized statement of principles governing criminal punishment and marked a major advance in criminological thought. Beccaria made an impassioned plea to humanize and rationalize the law and to make punishment more just and reasonable. He challenged the practices of the day, such as the death penalty and torture, arguing that such methods were ineffective in eliciting truthful confessions and only served to inflict unnecessary suffering on the accused. Beccaria advocated for individual dignity to be recognized and for punishments to be proportionate to the severity of the crime committed.

Beccaria was immediately celebrated as a profound new legal thinker. The American Revolution of 1775-1783 and French Revolution of 1789 led Beccaria's ideas to form the basis of modern criminal justice systems in the United States, France and beyond. They became the model for democracies around the world.

Some refer to Beccaria as the father of classicism, which was the **classical school** that pioneered criminological thought in the eighteenth century. Classicism defines the main object of study as **the offence** (and how to respond to it) rather than the causes of crime. Beccaria's belief that crime was a result of choice viewed the offender as being free-willed and calculating. However, the limitation with the classical school of thinking, some argued, was its disregard for the intent of the offender or the circumstances of the crime. As various criminologists argued over time, people do not always act as rational and autonomous beings.

The greatest happiness

Much like Beccaria, Jeremy Bentham championed the improvement of the criminal justice system. Bentham, an English philosopher and legal theorist, is known for developing the concept of "**utilitarianism**". His work, *An Introduction to the Principles of Morals and Legislation* (1789), introduced a philosophy of social control rooted in the principle of utility, aiming for "the greatest happiness of the greatest number".

Bentham argued that the morality of human actions should be judged on their impact on community happiness. He advocated assessing actions solely by their consequences, both for individuals and society, rather than their intentions. Bentham argued that no offence warranted capital punishment as it didn't deter crime effectively and instead inflicted unnecessary pain. He considered it more rational to seek alternatives that focused on rehabilitation and deterrence, aligning with his utilitarian principle of promoting overall societal well-being.

As founding figures of the classical school of criminology, Beccaria and Bentham established the principles for crime prevention strategies and emphasized the importance of just procedures, such as a fair trial and legal representation.

Legacy of the classical school

Thinkers like Beccaria and Bentham said that punishments should fit the crime and laws should be clear and known to everyone. They also encouraged crime prevention through deterrence and believed that people have the power to make rational choices. Their ideas helped shape the foundation of modern justice systems.

PROPORTIONATE PUNISHMENT

The concept that punishment should match the severity of the crime is still a fundamental principle in many legal systems. As such, a minor theft will result in a less severe punishment than a violent crime.

CLEAR LAWS AND DUE PROCESS

Individuals should be aware of their rights and the consequences of their actions. For example, police officers in the US must read suspects their legal rights before questioning them.

The classical school of criminology introduced ideas about fairness and reason that continue to be relevant today.

Adolphe Quetelet

During the mid-nineteenth century, a Belgian mathematician named Adolphe Quetelet made an important contribution to criminology by using statistics to understand patterns in crime. He wanted to figure out why people commit crimes and how society influences this.

Quetelet analyzed data about crime rates in France and noticed certain trends. He found that crime rates didn't just depend on individual choices but were also affected by the offender's background, including factors such as inequality, education, alcohol consumption and environment. Quetelet's key idea was that you could predict crime levels in a certain area or time based on these social factors.

This was a new way of thinking about crime – not just focusing on individual offenders but looking at the bigger picture of why crime happens in some places more than others. Quetelet's work proposed that crime isn't only about personal choices, but that "society itself contains the germs of all the crimes committed". This idea helped shape modern criminology and how we approach crime prevention and social policies.

Positivist school

Quetelet's statistical analysis of social trends inspired the development of the **positivist school** of criminology in the mid-to-late nineteenth century. This moved the focus of study away from the crime and onto **the offender**. By emphasizing the role of the environment, poverty and other societal conditions in crime rates, Quetelet's ideas laid the groundwork for considering external influences.

Unlike classicism, positivism viewed criminal behaviour as irrational and perhaps due to a problem that an individual has. The works of Cesare Lombroso, Enrico Ferri and Raffaele Garofalo explored the reasons behind criminal behaviour and suggested it was driven by factors beyond an individual's control:

- **Biological positivism** – looks at physical characteristics (such as height and strength), intelligence and other medical factors, such as hormone levels.

- **Psychological positivism** – looks at childhood experiences, mental illness and personality traits, such as introversion versus extroversion.

- **Social positivism** – looks at society as the cause of crime.

Cesare Lombroso and the hereditary criminal

In the 1870s, the Italian physician Cesare Lombroso claimed criminals often had features that distinguished them from law-abiding individuals. This theory argued for the existence of hereditary criminals. Lombroso viewed criminals as biological "throwbacks" to an earlier, more primitive stage of human evolution. He argued that criminal tendencies were genetic and that certain physical attributes increased the likelihood of committing crimes. He claimed to have seen associations between particular features and offences, such as:

- Swollen lips and eyelids, frailty, hunchback = rape.

- Bloodshot eyes, cold stare, strong jaw = murder.

- Thick and close eyebrows, small wandering eyes, sloping forehead = theft.

He claimed these distinctive physical traits, or "**atavistic**" **features**, signalled an inferior level of intellectual and moral development. This challenged the classical school of criminology, as he proposed that criminals were *not* driven by rational decision-making but were inherently predisposed. Criminals were born and not made.

According to Lombroso, criminals could not fit into society because they could not regulate their impulses. Their engagement in criminal activity was inevitable; they had no free will.

This theory of the born criminal dominated thinking about criminal behaviour until the early twentieth century. Though it is now discredited, Lombroso's theory played a pivotal role in shaping a new positivist perspective on crime, exploring connections between human biology, psychology and illegal behaviour. It also sealed Lombroso's legacy as the "father of criminology".

"SERIAL KILLER CHARM"

The notorious American serial killer Ted Bundy was known for his charm and handsome appearance. After his execution in 1989, Bundy's brain was studied for signs of physical abnormalities that could have explained his violent behaviour, but none were found. Bundy's case served as a reminder that appearances can be deceiving, and not all criminals fit the stereotypical image of what society might expect from violent offenders.

Enrico Ferri

Enrico Ferri took Lombroso's ideas further by suggesting that criminal behaviour isn't solely determined by an individual's biological make-up. In the late nineteenth century, Ferri argued that criminal actions result from a mixture of issues, including physiological traits, genetic predispositions, environmental conditions and social surroundings. Ferri's "Law of Criminal Saturation" proposed that any given criminal act is shaped by three factors:

- Physical or geographical

- Anthropological

- Psychological or social

A criminal was therefore a product of their physical and social environment, and crime could only be understood by considering combinations of factors. Ferri's research led him to conclude that a criminal should be treated as a product of existing life conditions. In his view, law enforcement policies should focus on crime *prevention* methods to remove these conditions, rather than punishment after the crime.

Natural crimes

Criminals are not found to be isolated factors in modern life, and the prevalence of crime is no fortuitous accident, but follows a law similar to that of mortality.
Richard L. Dugdale, sociologist

The Italian law professor Raffaele Garofalo is widely credited as being the first to coin the term *criminologia* in 1885. He used it to describe the emergence of criminal anthropology and to present his own ideas regarding illegal behaviour. Garofalo introduced the idea of "natural crimes" – actions that violate the fundamental values and collective sentiments shared by human beings, like murder or theft. These actions become universally recognized as crimes. This notion emphasized the common understanding of wrongdoing and helped shape ideas about the nature of criminal behaviour transcending cultural boundaries. Drawing on his own experience as a judge, Garofalo was pessimistic about the reformation of offenders.

Neoclassical school

Neoclassical criminology is a school of thought that emerged as a response to both classical and positivist criminological theories. Leading proponents tried to take account of free will, individual responsibility and external influences in explaining criminal behaviour. It recognized the existence of environmental, psychological and other **mitigating circumstances** that can inhibit free will and rationality. The school argues that when assessing criminal responsibility, there should be a degree of subjectivity, and punishments should be flexible to consider individual backgrounds.

Crimes committed by people who are less rational or who have less control over their actions should, according to the school, have a reduced penalty (including children or when there is extreme provocation). These ideas stemmed from several thinkers across the eighteenth to nineteenth centuries, including Gabriel Tarde (see page 40). Neoclassical ideas had a lasting impact on modern criminal justice systems, including individualized justice, consideration of age and separate juvenile systems, plus the use of sentencing guidelines to ensure consistency and proportionality.

SOCIAL CONTRACT THEORY

Social contract theory, as articulated by philosophers like Thomas Hobbes, John Locke and Jean-Jacques Rousseau, argues that individuals willingly enter a social contract with society, agreeing to abide by certain rules and laws in exchange for protection and order. Hobbes believed that, without government, life would be "solitary, poor, nasty, brutish, and short".

Individuals, by participating in the social contract, willingly accept the responsibility to adhere to the laws and norms of society because the punishments for violating those laws are theoretically fair and proportionate. This theory provided a philosophical foundation for neoclassical criminologists to reconcile the complexities of human behaviour and the justice system.

Determinism

Determinism is the philosophical idea that every event has a cause and free will is an illusion. In the context of criminology, it encompasses various theories that emphasize the role of external factors in shaping criminal behaviour, such as biological, psychological and environmental influences. While some aspects of determinism can be traced to earlier thinkers (such as Lombroso's focus on biology), the concept of determinism as a comprehensive perspective gained more prominence in the late nineteenth and early twentieth centuries.

THE "CRIME OF THE CENTURY"

In 1924, Nathan Leopold and Richard Loeb kidnapped and murdered a 14-year-old boy, with no apparent motive. Their defence lawyer, Clarence Darrow, argued that they could not have acted in any other way because "every human being is the product of the endless heredity back of him and the infinite environment around him". They avoided the death penalty and received a reduced prison term.

Émile Durkheim

In the 1890s, the French sociologist Émile Durkheim argued that even in a "society of saints" there would still be deviance. He believed crime serves various functions in society, like:

- Reinforcing social norms – when a person is charged with a crime, the boundaries of acceptable behaviour are visible to society.

- Promoting social change – if laws no longer reflect the shared values of a society, crimes can lead to legal reform.

- Enhancing social cohesion – when a community unites against a crime, it strengthens the sense of belonging.

Durkheim argued that societal conditions, like rapid social change, economic disparities and weakened social bonds can cause higher crime rates, and that criminal behaviour is influenced by social forces beyond an individual's control. His theory of **anomie**, linked to determinism, suggests that when there is a breakdown in societal norms and values, individuals might experience purposelessness and disconnection, leading to deviant behaviour.

Biological determinism

Building on the ideas of Cesare Lombroso (see page 28), several biological determinists gained significant attention during the late nineteenth and early twentieth centuries. This marked a time when scientific advancements and the study of human biology were on the rise. The idea that criminal behaviour could be linked to inherited traits and physical characteristics captured the imagination of scholars and the public alike. Some major figures include:

WILLIAM SHELDON

Sheldon developed somatotyping, a theory linking body physiques to personality traits and criminal tendencies. He believed specific body types were associated with criminal behaviour.

EARNEST HOOTON

Hooton advanced the concept of "anthropological criminology", focusing on the relationship between physical characteristics and criminality. He proposed that criminal behaviour was influenced by biological factors.

CHARLES GORING

Goring's research aimed to identify physical and hereditary traits associated with criminal behaviour. He conducted comparative studies of criminals and non-criminals to identify potential differences.

The proponents of biological determinism argued that factors such as genetics, physical traits and hereditary attributes played a significant role in predisposing individuals to criminal behaviour. While these theories have faced criticism, they contributed to shaping the broader discussion about the biological influences on criminality.

Psychological determinism

Psychological determinism suggests that our internal psyche steers our actions and determines whether we engage in criminal behaviour. During the early twentieth century, several thinkers played a central role in its development as an explanation for criminality, particularly Sigmund Freud. Freud's psychoanalytic theory explored how the unconscious mind and childhood experiences could drive criminal behaviour. Freud's contribution sparked discussions about the interplay between subconscious influences and criminal actions, leaving an enduring mark on the exploration of psychological determinants in criminology. Other notable ideas include:

UNDERLYING PSYCHOLOGICAL ISSUES

Psychiatrist William Healy focused on the psychological factors contributing to criminal behaviour, particularly in juvenile offenders. He emphasized the importance of addressing underlying psychological issues to prevent criminal actions.

EARLY INTERVENTIONS

August Aichhorn explored the role of childhood experiences and emotional disturbances in the development of criminal behaviour. He believed early interventions could address psychological factors contributing to delinquency.

PERSONALITY TRAITS

Hans Eysenck proposed a biological-psychological model of personality and criminal behaviour. He suggested certain personality traits, particularly extroversion and neuroticism, played a role in criminal tendencies.

SELF-CONTROL AND SOCIAL INFLUENCES

Walter Reckless introduced the concept of containment theory, which explained criminal behaviour as a result of both internal psychological factors and external pressures. He explored how self-control and societal influences interact in determining criminal actions.

Crime is contagious

French sociologist Gabriel Tarde viewed criminal behaviour as a product of **imitation** and **interaction** within society. His research in the late nineteenth century suggested that individuals observe and imitate the actions of others, leading to the spread of criminal acts like a ripple effect. When one person commits a crime, it serves as a model for others.

This process of imitation contributes to the growth of criminal actions. Tarde believed imitation was a means of learning and a fundamental mechanism by which societal norms and behaviours are established. He believed that societal dynamics play a significant role in shaping criminal behaviour, emphasizing the connection between individuals and their actions within the larger social context.

Tarde proposed that the social environment is crucial both in the development of criminal behaviour and its control. Tarde's theory underscores the idea that crime is a result of personal choices and is deeply intertwined with the actions of others. His influence can be seen in social learning theories that developed decades later (see page 96).

The spirit of youth

We may either smother the divine fire
in youth or we may feed it.
Jane Addams

Jane Addams was a pioneer social worker in the early twentieth century. She founded the Women's International League for Peace and Freedom in 1915 and was the second woman to receive the Nobel Peace Prize. She challenged Lombroso's theory of hereditary criminals (see page 28) by highlighting social factors in criminal behaviour. As a social worker in Chicago, she worked with impoverished communities and argued that poverty and social dislocation were key drivers of crime.

In her book, *The Spirit of Youth and the City Streets*, Addams stated that crime can be reduced by meeting the needs of young people by providing them with outdoor activity, practical education and exposure to the arts, claiming that delinquency is inevitable if society fails to provide for the "spirit of youth". Addams' theory expounded that crime isn't just about individual choices but also the environment in which those choices are made.

Community and crime

At the start of the twentieth century, the city of Chicago was a magnet for immigrants from European countries including Ireland, Italy and Poland. In 1860, its population was about 110,000; by 1910 it had grown to 2 million. The first ever department of Sociology at the University of Chicago used these communities to explore sociological theories of crime, which became known as the Chicago School of Criminology.

Research focused on the influence of social factors, neighbourhood conditions and social disorganization on criminal behaviour. They introduced the concept of **"social disorganization theory"**, showing how the environment shaped criminal behaviour. Research argued that those aforementioned impoverished and disorganized neighbourhoods fostered criminal behaviour as concentrated poverty, high levels of residential mobility and ethnic diversity weakened the social networks and increased the likelihood of crime. This perspective shifted attention from individual traits to community factors, laying the foundation for modern sociological criminology, while influencing urban planning and crime prevention strategies.

CHICAGO'S GANG ERA

The infamous mobster Al Capone ruled an empire of crime in Chicago during the 1920s, including gambling, bootlegging, "protection rackets" and murder. His ability to avoid justice until 1931 exposed law enforcement's limitations and forced researchers to rethink anti-crime strategies and the social drivers of criminal enterprises. Capone made criminologists think about new and better ways to understand and stop criminal behaviour, especially when it came to organized crime.

Learned behaviour

The sociologist Edwin Sutherland shook up the world of criminology during the 1920s and 1930s with his theory of **differential association**. Put simply, he proposed that if you hang out with lawbreakers, the chances are you'll become one too. He argued that our relationships inform our knowledge of – and affect our adherence to – social norms and laws. Just like you learn to ride a bike or cook a meal, you can also learn to be a criminal (and see it as "normal" behaviour). As such, illegality is learned through social interaction.

Sutherland shifted the focus from "what's wrong with you?" to "what happened to you?". He also coined the phrase "**white-collar crime**" to refer to offences committed by "a person of respectability and high social status in the course of his occupation" (see page 72). Sutherland's ideas challenged the notion that crime was just a problem of the underprivileged. His theories reshaped how we understand crime, emphasizing the role of social influences, peer groups and culture in shaping our paths.

MAJOR TOPICS
IN CRIMINOLOGY

In 2019, the reference book *Handbook of Crime Correlates* compiled over a century of research on criminal behaviour. It revealed over 100 risk factors, including gender, religion, personality traits, weapons access, alcohol and drug use, social status, geography and seasonality. These findings show how far criminology advanced during the twentieth century when it emerged as a social science with diverse strands of thinking.

The discipline evolved from the belief that criminals are born, not made, to adopt a multifaceted approach. It now explores criminal behaviour from numerous angles, including economic influences, political dynamics, intricate psychological motives, and the sociological forces and environments individuals inhabit. This chapter shows this evolution, highlighting the major topics that have fascinated criminologists for decades. As you explore the reasons why people break the law, you'll see that the answer is anything but simple. This complexity is one reason criminology is such a dynamic and evolving field; it seeks to unravel the intricate and ever-changing web of influences that contribute to criminal behaviour.

Biological theories

Biological theories of crime argue propensity to crime depends on the individual's biological nature, genetics, neurology or physical constitution. This perspective is not unique to early criminology scholars. Throughout history, societies have tried to identify criminals by physical traits, relying on superstition, stereotypes and bias. Ancient Greeks and Romans thought a person's character could be determined by their facial features (physiognomy), and medieval Europeans believed witches had distinctive marks. In 1786, the "father of American psychiatry", Dr Benjamin Rush, suggested a biological explanation for "morally deranged" behaviour and law breaking, prompting new biological theories of crime.

BUMPOLOGY

In the nineteenth century, phrenology was the belief that a person's character could be understood by their skull's shape. Supporters claimed that criminals could be identified by a particular series of bumps and that more "desirable" characteristics could be developed through mental training, such as reading and exposure to music and educational speakers.

Degeneration theory

In 1857, French psychiatrist Bénédict Morel introduced the **degeneration theory**, which proposed that criminal behaviour could be tied to inherited factors and a perceived decline in both physical and mental well-being. According to Morel, degeneration referred to an irreversible deterioration from a "higher" state to a "lower" one. This theory, also supported by social scientists like Richard Dugdale in the US (see page 53), suggested that self-destructive behaviour, like addiction and excessiveness, can cumulatively harm the nervous system, thereby weakening moral judgement and potentially leading to criminal acts. Crucially, this degeneracy was believed to be hereditary, passing through generations.

Although it has been largely discredited, the degeneration theory played a pivotal role in the early development of criminology. It redirected criminological focus towards biological explanations for criminal behaviour, spurring researchers to investigate potential connections between hereditary physical attributes and criminal tendencies. This shift marked a transition from moral philosophy to a more empirical, scientific approach to understanding crime.

EUGENICS

In 1883, Charles Darwin's half-cousin, Francis Galton, derived the term "eugenics" from the Greek *eugenes*, meaning "good in birth" or "good in stock". He believed desirable human qualities were entirely hereditary. His idea gave birth to the eugenics movement, which spread rapidly across Europe and the US. Harvard biologist Charles Davenport believed criminality resulted from a genetic defect known as "feeble inhibition", and that selective breeding could transform the human race (see page 52).

Atavistic theory

From the 1870s to early 1900s, Cesare Lombroso (see page 28) tried to build on the degeneration theory's ideas by identifying specific physical traits or anomalies associated with criminality. Lombroso developed the theory of **criminal anthropology**, asserting that certain physical characteristics could identify born criminals. He popularized the idea that criminals could be identified by their appearance.

> *We see in the criminal a savage man and, at the same time, a sick man.*
> **Cesare Lombroso**

Lombroso suggested that certain individuals possessed physical characteristics reminiscent of our distant, primitive ancestors – traits that he believed marked them as born criminals. Picture someone with a low sloping forehead, a prominent jaw and unusual cranial features. According to Lombroso, these were clear signs of an **"atavistic"** or throwback nature, indicating a more savage and criminal disposition. Lombroso's theory was groundbreaking but highly controversial. In response, he expanded his argument to include congenital illness and "degeneration".

Charles Goring and Enrico Ferri were some of the many scholars who challenged the validity of this theory in favour of more comprehensive and multifaceted ideas of criminal behaviour.

PRETTY PRIVILEGE

There was a law in medieval England that said if two persons fell under suspicion of crime, the "uglier" or "more deformed" was to be regarded as more probably guilty. More recently, a study in 2012 found that jurors are more likely to convict suspects deemed "ugly" than those considered attractive. As lead researcher Dr Sandie Taylor said, "perhaps justice isn't blind after all".

Bad seed

During the early twentieth century, nature prevailed over nurture in debates about the causes of crime. The "bad seed" concept held that criminals are born and not made because they have no moral values within themselves. To stop crime, action had to be directed at individuals not the state.

In the US, this meant sterilizing "unfit" or "genetically inferior" people to prevent the passage of "undesirable" traits. Between 1907 and 1963, over 64,000 individuals underwent forced sterilization in the US due to eugenics legislation. In the Supreme Court decision *Buck v. Bell* (1927), Justice Holmes wrote: "It is better for all the world, if instead of waiting to execute degenerate offspring for their crime... society can prevent those who are manifestly unfit from continuing their kind". Today, eugenics is discredited for its unethical and discriminatory practices. For criminologists like Nicole Hahn Rafter, born criminals were best understood as "cultural artifacts", not "hard scientific truth".

THE JUKES

The Jukes (a pseudonym) were an American family studied by sociologist Richard Dugdale in the late nineteenth century. While studying jails across New York, Dugdale found that one member of the family, named Max, was the ancestor of 76 convicted criminals, 18 brothel-keepers and 120 prostitutes. For decades, the family was used as an example of how hereditary factors shaped human behaviour and helped eugenicists argue for compulsory sterilization, segregation, lobotomies and even euthanasia against the "unfit".

Charles Goring

Atavistic, insane, savage, degenerate... one thing the criminologists will not let him be: he is not, he never is, say the Lombrosians, a perfectly normal human being.
Charles Goring

In 1913, the British criminologist Charles Goring published one of the most innovative studies of its time: *The English Convict: A Statistical Study.* To test Lombroso's hypothesis that criminals exhibit distinct physical traits associated with atavism, or a "born criminal" nature, Goring analyzed the data of 3,000 convicts.

His conclusion was clear: "There is no such thing as an anthropological criminal type." The physical and mental constitution were identical for both criminals and non-criminals of the same age, stature, class and intelligence. The rejection of the idea that criminal behaviour was primarily hereditary or biologically predetermined marked a pivotal moment in criminology. Goring's push for a broader understanding of the causes of crime played a crucial role in shaping modern criminology.

Hooton's theory on inferiority

For a quarter of a century, it seemed that Charles Goring had successfully discredited the previously dominant atavistic theory of criminals. Yet, in 1939, the narrative took an unexpected twist when American anthropologist Earnest Hooton revisited the subject. He embarked on a monumental undertaking, surveying nearly 14,000 inmates from ten diverse American states. He identified common characteristics reminiscent of Lombroso's findings, and claimed:

- Short, heavy men – commit assault, rape and sexual offences.

- Small men – commit theft and burglary.

- Tall, thin men – commit murder and robbery.

- Tall, heavy men – commit fraud.

He concluded that criminals were inferior to non-criminals for hereditary reasons, not situation or circumstance. Hooton's findings were heavily criticized for methodological flaws and overlooking the impact of poverty and malnourishment. As such, his study did not establish a definitive link between biology and criminality, leaving the debate unresolved.

Somatotypes theory

After the decline of ideas surrounding skull shape and ancestry, criminologists tried a different approach to connect criminal behaviour with biology: an individual's physique or body type. Most famously, the American psychologist William Sheldon (see page 36) suggested in the 1940s that everyone falls into one of three somatotypes (or constitutional types), with accompanying personality traits:

- **Endomorph** (soft and round) – wide hips and soft, rounded contours. Sociable, relaxed and expresses emotions verbally.

- **Ectomorph** (thin and slender) – narrow hips and prominent bones. Intelligent and sensitive, seeks privacy when under pressure.

- **Mesomorph** (muscular and athletic) – broad shoulders, narrow waist, and strong arms and legs. Brave, adventurous, aggressive and expresses emotions through physical action.

Sheldon believed that mesomorphs were more likely to be drawn to crime due to their need for adventure and their physical dominance from a young age. While researching "delinquent youths", he found a high proportion of mesomorphs and few endomorphs. His research was groundbreaking, spreading through the 1950s and used in attempts to characterize personality as late as the 1980s. It was, however, criticized for ignoring other potential factors like testosterone levels, being labelled a "troublemaker" from childhood (due to body size) or if a criminal lifestyle boosts muscle mass. He also failed to consider non-violent crimes, such as fraud, or that people's bodies change across their lifespan, perhaps because of profession or nutrition.

Two-path theory

Across the world, teenagers are known to take risks and dabble in deviant behaviour. The question that puzzled criminologists was why some continued down a path of delinquency while others became law-abiding citizens. In the 1990s, the American psychologist Terrie Moffitt developed a theory that suggested two distinct paths in life:

- **Adolescence-limited offenders** (AL) – "normal" deviance that occurs during puberty and is often influenced by environmental factors (like breaking curfew or trying alcohol before the legal age).

- **Life-course-persistent offenders** (LCP) – about 5-10 per cent of the population who exhibit antisocial behaviour early that then escalates with age. These individuals typically bite and hit others at age four and progress to crimes like shoplifting, selling drugs or violent offences. As Moffitt put it: "The underlying disposition remains the same, but its expression changes form as new social opportunities arise at different points in development."

Why do most teenagers become ALs? Because of a **"maturity gap"**. Moffitt explained how individuals reach the age of biological maturity and seek freedom, material goods and sexual contacts but also face restrictions imposed by society. Delinquent behaviour taps into the desirable "mature status". This disparity is the same for LCPs, but they start offending earlier and continue to commit crime because of added developmental factors like genetic predispositions, neuropsychological deficits, temperament and cognitive abilities.

Moffitt's **two-path theory** became one of the most influential of all developmental theories of antisocial behaviour. After decades of mystery, Moffitt argued for the complex interplay of biological and environmental factors that led people to be LCPs.

Political and economic theories

Criminology is deeply intertwined with politics because of its focus on crime, law and justice. This can be seen in many research areas, including:

- **Social control and power dynamics** – that control laws and their enforcement.

- **Justice and inequality** – issues of fairness, justice and societal inequality within the criminal justice system.

- **Policy and legislation** – crime-related policy decisions.

- **Public opinion** – public perceptions and media influence on crime and justice issues often have political implications, shaping policy and political agendas.

- **Advocacy and activism** – criminologists often engage in advocacy and activism to influence government policies.

Criminologists have developed several theories to explain how political and governmental processes influence ideas about crime. The theories relate to individual choice, conflict, societal labels and power dynamics. Understanding these concepts can help uncover the difference between political rhetoric and criminological analysis.

Deterrence theory

Deterrence theory suggests that people can be discouraged from committing crimes if they believe that the punishment for those crimes will be swift, certain and severe. The theory goes back a long way (see page 22). In the 1760s, Cesare Beccaria saw the purpose of punishment as two-fold:

1. To stop people from committing crime again (special/specific deterrence).

2. To stop others who know about the punishment from committing crime (general deterrence).

Laws that speed up the trial process or enforce severe punishments are likely to have been influenced by deterrence theory. It's also used by politicians to justify systemic changes such as increased policing or to boost arguments on issues like capital punishment, gun control and hate crime laws.

Capitalism and crime

In 1916, the Dutch criminologist Willem Adriaan Bonger did something quite revolutionary in the world of crime studies. Unlike the usual focus on biology and psychology, Bonger believed that society and money had a big role to play in why people commit crimes. He argued that when people didn't have enough money or when they were treated unfairly, they sometimes turned to crime to survive or protest against unfair treatment.

Bonger's Marxist-inspired analysis argued that crime was a reaction to a problem in society, not just something individuals did because they were born that way. Bonger believed that the economic system of capitalism could be a part of the problem because it encouraged selfishness. Bonger's ideas sparked a new way of thinking about crime, arguing that it wasn't just about "bad" individuals but also the world they lived in. This new perspective laid the foundation for what we now call critical criminology.

CRIMINOGENIC

Criminogenic means something that can make people more likely to commit crimes, like a neighbourhood with few jobs (economic hardship) and limited access to good schools (leading to a lack of opportunities). According to this theory, a criminogenic society is one where crime is inevitable due to its intrinsic nature.

Critical theories

Critical theories analyze our justice systems and reveal hidden structural issues that can drive criminal behaviour. In the 1920s, critical theories about crime found their home in the "Frankfurt School" in Germany (*Institut für Sozialforschung*), with ideas that explored the role of capitalism, class structures and inequality as drivers of criminal behaviour. Prominent scholars include:

MAX HORKHEIMER

Horkheimer was concerned with the concept of "**critical theory**" itself. He believed it should focus on social critique and the analysis of power structures, emphasizing the importance of understanding how culture and society shape individuals' perspectives and actions.

ERICH FROMM

Fromm emphasized the impact of societal norms and values on human behaviour, particularly in the context of alienation and conformity. He explored how individuals might turn to conformity or rebellion in response to social pressures.

JÜRGEN HABERMAS

Habermas' ideas marked the second generation of critical theories in the 1970s. He focused on the role of communication and rational discourse in society. He believed in the importance of public debate and reasoned dialogue as a means of achieving social change and resolving conflicts.

The common thread that flows through critical theories is the notion that social structures and justice systems are influenced by the powerful in society.

Encouraging egoism

Bonger's ideas and those of the Frankfurt School were heavily influenced by Karl Marx and Friedrich Engels, who argued that the capitalist economic system is criminogenic. In *The Communist Manifesto* of 1848, Marx and Engels argued that capitalist society, driven by economic inequality and exploitation, created conditions that pushed people towards criminal behaviour as a response to systemic injustices.

Bonger applied these ideas to criminology and argued that the individualistic focus of capitalism encouraged people to act out of self-interest, which weakened the social bonds that tied people together. For this reason, crime is not confined to the working classes. Bonger said that when wealthy and powerful individuals engaged in criminal activities, these actions often went unpunished or were seen as socially acceptable due to their privileged positions. For instance, the upper classes had more opportunities to engage in fraud and embezzlement, which often resulted in financial harm to others but were not treated as severely as street crimes.

The upper classes, Bonger argued, also shaped the laws and norms of society for their benefit, which influenced the way crimes were defined and punished. This perspective challenged the traditional view that crime was primarily a problem of the lower classes. Bonger emphasized the role of economic and social power in shaping the dynamics of criminal behaviour and justice.

CONFLICT CRIMINOLOGY

Critical theories include various perspectives, one of which is known as **conflict theory**. This views society not as one harmonious orchestra but as a cacophony of conflicting interests. Bonger's ideas on how economic factors influenced crime align with conflict theory, which focuses on power imbalances and societal inequalities as drivers of criminal behaviour.

Cultural conflict

In the 1930s, sociologist Thorsten Sellin's cultural conflict theory suggested that more complex societies lead to less consensus overall. He argued that "conduct norms" (the rules or norms of appropriate behaviour within society) are "products of social life". As societies grow and become more complicated, it's inevitable for different norms to develop and clash, especially if there's colonization, immigration or two cultures in the same space. The dominant culture decides the "crime norms" – what is inappropriate behaviour – and punishments.

CONFLICT AND UNITY

Sellin and other conflict theorists were influenced by the work of German sociologist Georg Simmel, who argued conflict is a necessary and natural part of society. He wrote in 1904, "As the cosmos requires '*Liebe und Hass*,' (love and hate) attraction and repulsion, in order to have a form, society likewise requires some quantitative relation of harmony and disharmony... in order to attain to a definite formation."

Conflict of interests

Criminologist George Vold's 1958 **group conflict** theory expanded the ideas of Sellin by presenting crime as a product of group struggle. Vold believed that most people are group-orientated and that society is made up of different groups engaging in ongoing power struggles – political, cultural or social. These group affiliations are said to be psychological rather than rational, and the conflicts that arise between groups strengthen the loyalty of members.

These group clashes within society give rise to criminal behaviour. Vold urged us to understand *how* such conflicts shape criminal activity rather than try to determine which group is "right" or "wrong".

This theory challenged researchers to study crime not just as the result of personal choices but as a reflection of broader societal tensions. By appreciating the profound impact of group dynamics on criminal behaviour, Vold encouraged a deeper understanding of how these collective conflicts influence the criminal landscape.

Consensus and coercion

Whether they realize it or not, people are inevitably involved in intergroup struggles over who shall have what resources in a finite world.
Austin Turk

In 1969, the American criminologist Austin Turk argued that crime and social control should be viewed as part of a broader struggle for power and resources in society. He claimed society is characterized by conflict between various groups seeking to establish control over one another, and that social order is based on a consensus–coercion balance preserved by key authorities, like those in government or religion.

His work encouraged criminologists to analyze crime and justice within the context of social conflict and to question the fairness and legitimacy of existing legal and criminal justice systems. Turk's conflict theory has had a lasting impact on the field, influencing the study of crime and social control from a critical and power-orientated perspective.

Economic inequality

The rich get richer and the poor get prison.
Jeffrey Reiman, philosopher

Many criminologists have studied the impact of income inequality on crime levels. Unlike poverty, which broadly means a lack of material items needed for a basic level of existence, economic inequality is a discrepancy in levels of material possessions between groups in society. A country can be rife with poverty but have little economic inequality, and vice versa.

Academics Richard Wilkinson and Kate Pickett found that unequal rich countries, such as the UK and the US, have much worse outcomes across areas including health, drug abuse, imprisonment and violence compared with countries with the lowest economic inequality, such as the Scandinavian nations and Japan. As an interesting variance, a Belgian study found no significant relationship between income inequality and violent crime but instead income inequality had a strong effect on property crime. Criminologists agree that income inequality is an important contributor to criminal behaviour, impacting both street crime and white-collar crime.

White-collar crime

Edwin Sutherland's introduction of the term "white-collar crime" in the 1940s transformed criminology (see page 44). Until then, the discipline reflected the mass media depiction of crime as a world of masks, guns and dark alleys. Sutherland exposed the hidden offences occurring at the highest levels of society that were often overlooked or treated leniently by the criminal justice system. This was a new kind of villain – well-dressed executives, bankers and professionals who used their positions and knowledge to swindle, cheat or commit fraud.

These crimes didn't leave physical scars but they could ruin lives and economies. Corporate crime, for example, involves activities carried out by company employees for corporate rather than personal benefit. It comes in many forms, including false accounting, bribery, corruption or misappropriation of funds. The scale can be enormous; unauthorized trading by the derivatives broker Nick Leeson in 1995 caused Baring's Bank to lose £827 million.

PINTO EXPLOSIONS

In the 1970s, the Ford Motor Company sold the Pinto model of car in the US with the knowledge that it was dangerous due to a flaw in its design. An internal cost-benefit analysis revealed there would be a substantially higher cost to fix the design flaw than deal with any potential legal damages due to collisions and loss of life. An article in the investigative magazine *Mother Jones* in 1977 argued that Ford had caused the deaths of 500–900 people. In 1978, a crash that involved the deaths of three people led to a grand jury indicting Ford on three counts of reckless homicide – the first time a company had ever faced such a charge. Ford was found not guilty. It wasn't until July 1980 that Ford stopped producing Pintos.

White versus blue

Why are white-collar crimes treated less harshly than street crimes? It's a question that has puzzled many criminologists, especially as the financial cost of white-collar crime is far higher than losses caused by street criminals. In the early 2020s, white-collar crime was estimated to cost victims in the US $300 billion annually, compared with the damages incurred by street crime at $16 billion.

The criminologist Hermann Mannheim wrote in 1946, "The failure to take adequate actions against white-collar, middle-class and corporate wrongdoers sends out wrong messages to society as a whole." To understand the reasons, criminologists emphasize the distinguishing features of white-collar crime versus street crime (also known as blue-collar crime):

WHITE-COLLAR CRIME (e.g. money laundering, insider trading, tax evasion)	BLUE-COLLAR CRIME (e.g. assault, theft, drug offences)
Considered "victimless" – no specific individual is targeted or deliberately harmed (e.g. the state is harmed by tax evasion). Often involves complicated plans for hiding operations or stealing money	Street crimes like murder threaten us personally and violate our sense of security
Usually non-violent	Can involve violence or the threat of it – physical violence often results in punitive measures
Motivation is to maximize profits and accumulate capital	Not always financially motivated
Requires in-depth knowledge about financial systems – proving guilt is difficult and requires a paper trail involving thousands of documents	Does not require specialist knowledge and proving guilt can be straightforward

Who makes the rules?

Since the 1960s, criminologists have explored the way social and economic power dynamics influence the definition and enforcement of criminal behaviour, with a focus on the role of the upper classes. As sociologist Richard Quinney put it, the powerful group in society have the power to create the law, which he described as "the formulation of criminal definitions", and they are also uniquely placed to *apply* the law and its sanctions because of their control over law enforcement. He described this as "the application of criminal definitions".

In this way, according to Quinney, the powerful elite determine the content and scope of the criminal law so that it reflects their personal values and interests rather than the common interests of society. Where the behaviour of less powerful groups does not match the norms of the elite, it is considered deviant or criminal. Austin Turk developed this argument by saying that laws are more likely to be *enforced* if they reflect the values of society's authority group.

Benefiting the elite

It is commonly believed that laws have a double standard: the privileged elite escape justice for their crimes while the less fortunate face severe consequences. In the late twentieth century, several criminologists shed light on this apparent bias. William Chambliss argued, "at the heart of the Capitalist system lies the protection of private property and other ruling-class interests", which determines which acts are defined as criminal by the state.

Steven Box emphasized how only some types of avoidable death are illegal; criminal law often fails to include "deaths resulting from acts of negligence, such as employers' failure to maintain safe working conditions; or deaths which result from governmental agencies giving environmental health risks a low priority".

Laureen Snider argued that capitalist states are reluctant to regulate large capitalist concerns and threaten profitability. These theories offer a glimpse into the believed mechanisms that allow the elite to navigate the law with ease, often escaping its full force, while the less advantaged face the brunt of justice.

Crimes of the powerful

Professor Frank Pearce extended the ideas of conflict theory with his groundbreaking book, *Crimes of the Powerful*. He explored the relationship between power, crime and the state, and how societal inequalities and structures create a fertile ground for criminal behaviour.

Pearce scrutinized the role of the state in maintaining a power imbalance and how it can maintain or reduce criminal behaviour. His insights encouraged criminologists to question authority, explore the social roots of crime and champion fairness within the criminal justice system.

BHOPAL TRAGEDY

In 1984, the population of the Indian city of Bhopal was devastated by the release of a cocktail of gases by Union Carbide India Limited, a majority owned subsidiary of the American multinational Union Carbide Corporation. The tragedy inspired Pearce's book *Toxic Capitalism: Corporate Crime and the Chemical Industry*, written to critically analyze corporate power and make sense of how such incidences occur.

A man's world

For most of its history, criminology's scholars were predominantly male and studies focused on men's criminal activities. Typically, female offenders were assumed to be already included within theories or they were dealt with extremely briefly. The first person to explore women's criminal activity was Cesare Lombroso (see page 28). His belief that criminals were "genetically inferior" humans extended to men and women, and he suggested women who committed crimes were unnaturally masculine. Scholars that came after Lombroso claimed to exclude female offenders from their work because they were "statistically insignificant" in comparison with male offenders.

ANDROCENTRISM

Androcentrism is the practice – conscious or otherwise – of placing a masculine point of view at the centre of one's worldview, culture and history, thereby culturally marginalizing femininity. In 1988, criminologists Kathleen Daly and Meda Chesney-Lind wrote that criminology was awakening from its "androcentric slumber" thanks to feminist critiques.

Feminist criminologies

In the 1970s, gender began to be taken seriously in criminological thinking. In reaction to the general disregard of women, researchers started to explore if there were different ways that men and women commit crimes and to understand the reasons for their criminal involvement. The four main perspectives are outlined below:

- **Liberal/liberation feminism** – believes men and women are equal and should be treated the same way by the criminal justice system. The problem with this perspective is its failure to consider how women's needs and risk factors differ from men.

- **Marxist** – believes in equality and views the gender distinction as a form of exploitation perpetuated by capitalism. Women's unequal access to jobs results in them being disproportionately involved in property crime and illegal sex work.

- **Radical** – views the existing social structure as patriarchal. Women's criminal behaviour can be explained by men's control over women, such as through prostitution or drug and human trafficking. Violence against women can only be addressed by removing the existing patriarchal social structure.

- **Socialist** – views the existing social structure as oppressive against women because of the patriarchy and capitalism. Differences in power and class can explain gendered differences in offending, especially male violent crime.

GENDER, NOT SEX

Feminist theories focus on gender as a socially constructed concept rather than the biological category of sex (which was the focus of previous scholars like Lombroso).

Masculinization theory

Freda Adler, a pioneering feminist criminologist, introduced the **masculinization theory** in the 1970s. She challenged stereotypes by suggesting that as women gained social and economic equality with men, their participation in crime would also become more similar to that of men, leading them to engage in typically "male" criminal behaviour, such as violent offences. The criminologist Rita Simon agreed; she suggested that women's lower rates of participation in criminal activity until the 1970s could be explained by their confinement to domestic roles and by discrimination that limited career aspirations.

This theory emphasized the importance of considering societal changes and gender dynamics when understanding women's involvement in crime. It has faced criticism, including a failure to predict trends or shifts in the crimes women would commit, its focus on economic factors and for its binary view of gender. Despite these criticisms, Adler's work paved the way for the exploration of changing gender patterns in criminal behaviour. She challenged the widespread assumption that women's criminality would always be different from men's.

Ethics of care

Cultural feminism emphasizes biological differences between men and women. In 1976, psychologist Carol Gilligan suggested that men and women should not be treated equally because their motivations for committing crimes are different. She believed women view morality through a lens of relationships, compassion and responsibility to others – what she called the "ethics of care". Men base morality on rights, laws and universally applied principles: the "ethics of justice". Other research supported some of Gilligan's ideas, but she was criticized for ignoring societal expectations and reinforcing traditional notions of femininity.

DIVERSITY OF WOMEN

Postmodern feminists have emphasized the fluidity and complexity of gender identities. They believed that the criminal justice system should be more inclusive to diverse gender experiences. In the twenty-first century, intersectional feminists have considered how women can experience multiple inequalities. Their research explores how gender intersects with other inequalities that can influence criminal behaviour (or the risk of victimization), including race, class, ethnicity, ability and sexual orientation.

Gender roles

Criminological theories have suggested that social ideas about "masculinity" are important in criminal behaviour, and feminist research has indicated that boys and men will engage in this behaviour if they are unable to "do their gender" through legitimate means. In his book, *Masculinities and Crime*, sociologist James W. Messerschmidt proposed that men *construct* masculinity in specific social situations, and those who don't have access to hegemonic masculinity may resort to crime. For instance, he suggested that men working on a shop floor may assert their masculinity by humiliating women or stealing, while their managers may do so by expecting sex from female assistants or resorting to white-collar crime if profits fall and their reputation is threatened.

A "REAL MAN"

Hegemonic masculinity refers to a societal pattern in which stereotypically male traits are idealized as the masculine cultural ideal. In North American and European cultures, this includes heterosexuality, risk-taking behaviours, physical prowess and sporting skill.

Labelling theory

The person becomes the thing he is described as being.
Frank Tannenbaum, historian

Labelling theory, which found its footing in the 1960s and 1970s, focused not on why individuals commit crimes but how society labels and reacts to those who do. The pioneer of this was sociologist Howard S. Becker. He suggested that individuals are not inherently "criminal" but become so when society applies the label of "deviant" or "criminal" to their actions.

Becker's idea suggested that these labels, often imposed by those in positions of power, can have profound consequences. Once labelled, individuals may internalize these roles, leading to a self-fulfilling prophecy of continued criminal behaviour. Under this theory, a boy who is labelled a "troublemaker" may take more action to live up to that label, behaving in a way that he would otherwise not have done. The label makes the individual feel that there is no opportunity to change, and thus, they fulfil the prophecy of being a "troublemaker" by acting the way the label suggests.

Shame and social control

Labelling theory shook the very foundations of traditional criminological thought. It urged researchers to question the fairness of a system that often stigmatizes and perpetuates criminality. In the 1980s and 1990s, the theory developed in three major directions:

MODIFIED LABELLING THEORY

Sociologist Bruce Link introduced the concept of "modified labelling", emphasizing the importance of individual perceptions and reactions to labels. He argued that the negative consequences of labelling are not uniform for everyone; they depend on how individuals interpret and respond to being labelled. Link highlighted the role of mental health and self-concept in the labelling process, suggesting that if individuals can mitigate the harm caused by negative labels through resilience and positive self-perception, they are less likely to continue engaging in criminal behaviour.

REINTEGRATIVE SHAMING THEORY

Criminologist John Braithwaite introduced the idea that society can respond to criminal behaviour with shaming that is not stigmatizing but rather aims to reintegrate the offender into the community. This approach emphasized the importance of repairing the social bonds disrupted by criminal acts. By promoting empathy and support rather than stigmatization, reintegrative shaming seeks to discourage repeat offending and foster a sense of responsibility and belonging.

DIFFERENTIAL SOCIAL CONTROL THEORIES

Sociologists Ross L. Matsueda and Karen Heimer argued that variations in social control influence criminal behaviour. If someone has less guidance or social control, which can happen when they're struggling economically, they might be more likely to break the law.

Labelling theory deals not just with the actions of individuals but the judgements and labels society places on them. This has sparked conversations about justice and stigma.

Radical theory

Radical criminology emerged as a counter-narrative to mainstream theories of crime and justice. The work of Ian Taylor, Paul Walton and Jock Young challenged the idea that crime is solely a result of personal choices and instead pointed to systematic injustices as the driving forces behind criminal behaviour. Radical criminologists argue that crime is a result of structural factors, such as poverty, racism and inequality, and that criminal justice policies and practices are often used to maintain the status quo and perpetuate social control. It's a perspective that encourages alternative paths to justice and equality.

One of the key concepts is **"law as a weapon"**. This refers to the way power relations and social control are maintained in society through the law and law enforcement practices. For example, these theories may argue that criminalizing drug use may target disadvantaged communities disproportionately, instead of tackling underlying social and economic factors that contribute to it.

Redefining crime

Radical criminologists challenged the traditional definition of crime, shifting the focus from legalities to the violation of fundamental human rights. Proponents believed that they should not limit their research to the legal definitions of crime because the ruling class decided these definitions. As Jeffrey Reiman put it: "the criminal justice system is a carnival mirror that presents a distorted image of what threatens us."

By rejecting strict legal definitions, scholars would avoid "state-imposed" restrictions on the study of crime and criminal behaviour. In this new perspective, crimes extend beyond mere legal offences and include actions like environmental pollution, exploitative practices, assaults on indigenous communities, unfair labour and business practices, and exploitation of vulnerable populations. Traditionally these have been overlooked in criminology. This focus on human rights has broadened the scope of inquiry to include crimes by the state and support the growing call by academics to practise and participate in political struggles themselves.

The new criminology

In 1973, Ian Taylor, Paul Walton and Jock Young co-authored the influential book *The New Criminology*. The three British criminologists presented crime as a product of capitalism, inequality and social structures. They believed that criminology "over-identified" with the work of social control agencies like the police, government and the judiciary and neglected the social and political context of crime. They argued that criminal behaviour has a structural origin; the root cause is how society is organized at the institutional level, particularly capitalism. Their considerations included dismantling the capitalist system and envisioning a more equitable society.

Other criminologists inspired by these ideas highlighted the criminogenic function of the state. These critical criminologists sought to explain the media's role in orchestrating public panics about crime and deflecting concerns away from the social problems that emanate from capitalism. In 1978, during a "crisis of capitalism" (an economic recession), Marxist sociologist Stuart Hall argued that the British state and media deliberately created a moral panic about crime. In Hall's view, by falsely claiming that there was a wave of street crime committed by Black people, the state divided the working class and encouraged people to blame immigrants and Black people for unemployment, thereby preventing political activism and radical political change.

POPULAR CULTURE

The work of artists and writers outside academia have been part of the development of critical criminology. Fyodor Dostoevsky's novel *Crime and Punishment* and George Bernard Shaw's book *Doctor's Delusions: Crude Criminology and Sham Education* explored ideas about human greed, exploitation and oppression as alternatives to prevailing views of crime and depicted social discontent against those in power.

Psychological theories

Psychological theories of crime suggest that an individual turns to crime in response to unconscious mental processes resulting from early childhood experiences and that social behaviour is learned. These ideas trace their origins to the late nineteenth and early twentieth centuries when scholars like Sigmund Freud began exploring the link between human psychology and criminal behaviour. Initially, psychological theories focused on individual traits and unconscious motivations as drivers of crime. Over time, they started to consider how social and environmental factors can also shape criminal behaviour.

These theories have broadened the scope of criminology to include the psychological dimensions of crime. They have influenced research, criminal justice policies and interventions. By recognizing the role of cognition, personality and social learning, psychological theories seek a more holistic understanding of why individuals engage in criminal activities and how society can respond effectively.

Psychodynamic perspective

Sigmund Freud, often hailed as the father of psychoanalysis, was a trailblazing Austrian neurologist. He proposed that crime could be traced to unresolved conflicts buried deep within the human psyche, like treasure chests of repressed desires and traumatic experiences. These inner struggles, he argued, could manifest in criminal behaviour so individuals could cope with their inner turmoil. While Freud did not specifically formulate a theory of crime, his insights into the role of unconscious motivations, unresolved conflicts and inner struggles in shaping human actions have had a lasting influence on criminology.

PERSONALITY/SELF

Freud believed that everyone has instinctive drives (called the "id") that demand gratification. Moral and ethical codes (called the "superego") regulate these drives, and adults later develop a rational personality (called the "ego") that mediates between the id and superego. Criminal behaviour, Freud said, arises from conflict between the id, ego and superego, with the superego ultimately failing.

Behavioural theory

In the 1940s, the work of behavioural psychologist B. F. Skinner transformed our understanding of criminal behaviour. He thought the best way to understand human behaviour is to look at what causes an action and, most importantly, the *consequence* (punishment or reinforcement) of the action. He concluded:

- Learning occurs when behaviour is followed by consequences.

- Behaviour is shaped through reinforcement (positive or negative) and punishment.

- Individuals may engage in criminal acts if they perceive rewards or reinforcements for doing so, like money or power. Conversely, punishment or negative consequences may deter criminal behaviour.

This behavioural theory, often called **"operant conditioning"**, led to the development of behavioural interventions within the criminal justice system, such as cognitive behavioural therapy and contingency management programmes. This was aimed at reducing reoffending and addressing the root causes of criminal behaviour.

SKINNER BOX

A "Skinner box" refers to a controlled environment used for conducting animal experiments. Within this enclosure, the animal is typically isolated and interacts with levers or other equipment. When the animal presses a lever or acts a certain way, it may receive rewards or punishments. These experiments played a pivotal role in shaping Skinner's theories.

Social learning theory

Fortunately, most human behaviour is learned observationally through modelling: from observing others one forms an idea of how new behaviours are performed.
Albert Bandura, psychologist

Social learning theory (SLT) drew inspiration from Skinner's behavioural theory but adapts it. Picture a scenario where you witness someone being rewarded for breaking the rules, or you see their actions glorified in the media. SLT argues that these observations will influence your own choices, steering you towards criminal acts.

A leading advocate of SLT was Albert Bandura, who emphasized the role of observational learning and social influences in the development of criminal behaviour. He suggested that individuals imitate the behaviour of others, especially if they perceive rewards for said behaviour. SLT challenges the idea that we're born with criminal tendencies. Instead, it suggests we *absorb* criminal behaviour like sponges through observation and interaction. SLT helps criminologists understand how to prevent crime. By offering positive role models and promoting prosocial behaviours, the cycle of crime transmission can be broken.

Self-control theory

Self-control theory, first developed by criminologists Michael R. Gottfredson and Travis Hirschi, suggests that self-control (the ability to inhibit impulses and delay gratification to obtain a later reward) is an important predictor of crime. Studies show that self-control is formed early in life through "supportive parenting". Those with low self-control often seek immediate gratification, take risks and have limited long-term planning. Self-control is reduced if a person is socially excluded and believes that their actions have no impact upon future acceptance. Fatalism regarding the future also increases the acceptability of risk-taking, including crime.

BOBO DOLL EXPERIMENT

A groundbreaking study showed that children learn aggressive behaviours that they observe in adults. Children watched adults attack a Bobo doll (a clown-faced inflatable toy). To create frustration in the children, after 2 minutes of playing with various toys, they were told that they could only play with the Bobo doll and other "aggressive toys". Children who saw the attack mimicked the behaviour with the doll when given the opportunity.

Rational choice theory

In films, characters are often sorted into two groups: "heroes" or "villains". This simplistic view suggests that the "villains" commit crime and the "heroes" follow the law. For much of the twentieth century, criminology theories took a similar approach to society, but in the 1960s, economist Gary S. Becker theorized a new economic model of crime. He shifted the focus from character to available individual choices. Becker believed that people make rational choices regarding crime based on calculations. As such, there are no "heroes" or "villains", just people weighing up the potential economic benefits and costs of criminal activities.

In Becker's model, a criminal act is preferred if the expected benefits from committing an offence are higher than its costs (including direct material costs, psychological costs and expected punishment costs), including the price of pursuing any legal alternatives. While certain aspects of character are relevant, like taking risks or impulsiveness, criminal activity represents a choice available to everyone. Becker's ideas contributed to the understanding of how economic factors influence criminal decision-making.

Cognitive theory

How do you know the difference between right and wrong? Psychologist Lawrence Kohlberg developed one of the best-known theories on this question. He proposed a six-stage model of moral development, where individuals progress through stages of reasoning and ethical understanding:

PRECONVENTIONAL MORALITY

Ages 0–9. Individuals focus on self-interest (Stage 1: Obedience and Punishment) and personal gain (Stage 2: Individualism and Exchange).

CONVENTIONAL MORALITY

Older children, adolescents and most adults. Individuals conform (Stage 3: Good Interpersonal Relationships) and abide by societal rules (Stage 4: Maintaining Social Order).

POST-CONVENTIONAL/PRINCIPLED MORALITY

Only 10–15 per cent of adults in all populations. Individuals prioritize social contracts (Stage 5: Social Contract and Individual Rights) and universal ethical principles (Stage 6: Universal Principles). Post-conventionalists place their moral evaluation of a situation above social conventions.

Personality theories

A common question in early criminology tackled why some people were more prone to commit crimes. Personality theories have helped to determine if certain characteristics can predict or explain criminality. Psychologist Gordon Allport's **trait theory** suggested that personality develops like a series of building blocks, referred to as "traits". He found 4,500 personality traits within one English-language dictionary, which he split into three categories:

- Cardinal – traits that summarize a person entirely, like narcissism.

- Central – words used to describe a person, such as quiet, generous and funny.

- Secondary – only relevant in certain situations, like being aggressive in traffic.

The theory has been influential in criminology, with studies showing that individual personality traits represent a predictor of criminal behaviour regardless of gender, race, age or geographical location. Psychologist Hans Eysenck suggested that criminal behaviour is more likely in individuals who display high levels of extroversion, neuroticism and psychoticism, which he called "super traits".

Psychopathy and antisocial personality disorder

For centuries, people have associated crime with mental disorder, especially violent offences. Some early criminologists suggested that crime itself is a symptom of mental disorder. A 2009 study found over 100 films depicting people suffering from psychosis as "psychokillers".

According to psychologist Robert Hare, people are either psychopaths (characterized by traits such as manipulation and lack of remorse) or non-psychopaths, and the psychopathic minority commit most of society's crimes. While there is no conclusive proof of a link between mental disorder and crime, studies show that psychopathy and antisocial personality disorder (APD) are risk factors for criminal behaviour. A person with APD has a pattern of manipulating, using and violating the rights of others without remorse or guilt. The link between APD and crime is strong. Studies show its high prevalence within prison populations, ranging from about half to three-quarters of incarcerated people.

Most criminologists agree that mental disorders cannot explain why large numbers of people across society commit crimes. In most cases, offending is not a result of a mental disorder.

Age

One of the few facts agreed on by criminologists is that younger people, particularly males, are more likely to engage in criminal activity than older people. Research consistently shows that criminal activity peaks during adolescence and early adulthood, then declines with age. This is referred to as the **"age-crime curve"**. The potential causes for this trend are hotly debated. Some theories suggest that young people engage in crime because of a failure to learn appropriate behaviour and value systems; they have experienced "inadequate socialization". This is often defined as poor parenting, lack of supervision and an absent parent (especially a father).

Others suggest a lack of discipline or a flawed education system is to blame. In 2013, sociologists Elizabeth Brown and Mike Males studied arrests in California and concluded that the adolescent peak in rates of offending was due to differences in economic status. Youngsters, they argued, offend more than adults simply because they are poorer than adults.

STREET DISTURBANCES

Law enforcement officers often take a hard line against street disturbances, like riots, robberies or political demonstrations – acts that are often committed by younger people. One often-highlighted example is that in the 1960s, England was known for clashes between "mods" and "rockers". British criminologist Sandra Walklate has argued that there is hypocrisy in this approach because of clear similarities between the "rude, and belligerent behaviour" between debating politicians and "lads who shout, whistle and jostle" on street corners. The only difference, according to this argument, is their "public and political acceptability".

Feeling the strain

Imagine you're at a party, and there's a tempting bowl of your favourite snack in the centre of the room. You haven't eaten for hours and you desperately want some. But there's a catch: you can't reach the bowl because you're stuck in a corner.

Criminologist Robert K. Merton presented a theory to describe this kind of situation on a larger social scale. Known as **strain theory**, Merton proposed that when people want something badly, like success or a better life, but lack legitimate means to get it, they might resort to "short cuts" or breaking rules. The pressure of wanting something but not having a fair chance builds up and eventually results in criminal behaviour.

Strain theory posits why some people at the party might take extreme measures to get to that snack. People turn to crime when there is a disconnect between societal goals – or even demands (like wealth and material possessions) – and the means available to achieve them (like employment and education).

Anomie theory

Merton's strain theory focused on a person's response to the strain between goals and means. He developed it further by examining the societal conditions that *create* this strain and put forward his own **anomie theory**. The concept of anomie was created by Émile Durkheim to describe the state of social chaos and normlessness that arises in times of major upheaval, such as an economic recession (see page 35). Unlike Durkheim, Merton believed the state of anomie is a constant in society because structural conditions generate an ongoing state of normlessness. Anomie isn't merely a response to temporary social breakdowns but is an inherent part of societal dynamics. It disproportionately affects individuals at the lower end of the socioeconomic ladder.

Merton's ideas provide an alternative explanation for why people might turn to deviant behaviour when they feel legal paths to success are closed. His insights have greatly impacted criminology, arguing for an intricate relationship between society's structures and individuals' choices.

Merton's influence

During the 1950s and 1960s, Merton's strain theory dominated criminology and was considered one of the most influential formulations of deviance. By the 1970s, however, it had fallen out of favour. This was mainly due to its assumption that everyone in the US (and other capitalist societies) was pursuing the same goal of material wealth and paid little attention to different cultures and subcultures. Merton's theories primarily linked strain to economic success goals. Critics suggested that it overlooked other aspirations like social status, respect or personal fulfilment, which can lead to deviant behaviour when obstructed. Some believed that Merton overlooked the role of social structures and power, like the impact of big business on crime.

Despite the criticisms, Merton's ideas have influenced subsequent research and developments in criminology. Scholars built upon his work, addressing some of the criticisms and adapting the theories to better fit evolving social contexts. Researchers have explored new avenues within strain theory, such as the study of multiple strains and coping mechanisms.

General strain theory

Merton's strain theory was developed by criminologist Robert Agnew, who proposed that individuals are drawn to crime when they experience strain or stress because of:

- **Failure to achieve goals** – when people are unable to attain desires such as success, wealth or respect.

- **Removal of positive stimuli** – if individuals lose something they value, like a job or a loved one.

- **Introduction of negative stimuli** – experiencing negative events, like abuse or discrimination.

The range of possible strains, particularly on young people, goes far beyond financial pressures. Agnew's **general strain theory** recognized the importance of emotions like anger, frustration and depression as drivers of criminal behaviour and supported the development of more comprehensive crime prevention strategies. It also underscored the importance of social support and coping mechanisms in reducing the likelihood of criminal acts in response to strain.

Social bulimia

Merton's anomie theory inspired Jock Young's idea of a "bulimic society". Young argued that rising crime rates resulted from three decades of policies that excluded more members from society. Those considered "the difficult and the dangerous" were welcomed by society in theory as part of drives for diversity but were rejected in practice.

Society had become fractured and fraught with high levels of unemployment. In later works, Young summarized this idea as "a bulimic society where massive cultural inclusion is accompanied by systematic structural exclusion". Culturally, the poor and wealthy were all fed the same consumerist and materialistic message, but structurally, financial rewards were irrational and not reflective of people's hard work. It is not the fact of deprivation that leads to crime, but the *feeling* of deprivation that arises from social comparisons (feeling "poor" relative to others around you). Young also pointed out that ethnic minorities, inner-city residents and the poor (in place of the rich) were usually the victims of street crimes like mugging and theft.

LEFT REALISM

Young was known as a "left realist" – one of several British criminologists, including Richard Kinsey and John Lea, who arose in the 1980s and believed in the reform of society. They argued that crimes other than white-collar crimes were a serious problem that needed to be tackled – but not with longer sentences or more prisons. Left realists focused on other ways to reduce crime, such as improved police relationships with the community.

Deviant subcultures

Criminologist Albert Cohen presented a theory of deviant subcultures. Cohen argued that individuals from lower socioeconomic backgrounds, who face strains and disconnections from mainstream values and opportunities, may develop their own subcultures as a response. These subcultures often invert conventional norms, celebrating values opposite to those of larger society. For instance, people can gain status and recognition through delinquency, providing an alternative pathway to gaining respect and identity. Cohen paid particular attention to working-class boys, who he believed were inadequately prepared for the "middle-class measuring rod" of school. The theory highlighted the role of social class and cultural values in shaping criminal behaviour among young people.

Criminologists Marvin Wolfgang and Franco Ferracuti progressed these ideas with their **subculture of violence theory**. They observed that some subcultures (in predominantly low-income communities) view violence and aggression as an acceptable way to respond to a perceived personal attack. Aggression is normalized and valued to gain status and respect, resulting in high rates of interpersonal violence.

Crime in the city

In 1829, geographer Adriano Balbi and lawyer André-Michel Guerry created the world's first crime map, revealing a trend that persists to this day – more crime tends to happen in urban areas than in rural regions. It's a pattern observed consistently across various countries. Criminologists have delved into these geographical variations, examining offences between countries, provinces, cities, communities and even individual streets.

The early twentieth century marked a milestone in this research. The Chicago School conducted pioneering crime studies primarily focused on cities and large urban areas. Urban ecology theories in criminology scrutinize how the social and physical characteristics of urban environments influence patterns of crime and delinquency. These theories explore the intricate relationships between neighbourhood dynamics, social structures and criminal behaviours, shedding light on the complex interplay between urbanization and crime rates.

Neighbourhood disorder

The relationship between neighbourhood disorder and crime was proposed by several criminologists during the 1980s-1990s. One of the most renowned theories is **broken windows**, developed by criminologists James Wilson and George Kelling. They suggested that crime increases when there are visible signs of disorder, like broken windows, litter or graffiti. Wilson and Kelling believed that neglect in neighbourhoods signals a lack of social control, leading to more offences and even more serious crimes. Other notable theories include:

- **Robert J. Sampson and William Julius Wilson** – concentrated poverty and social disorganization in disadvantaged neighbourhoods contribute to higher crime.

- **Ralph B. Taylor** – a poor physical environment, including abandoned buildings and vacant lots, is conducive to criminal activity.

- **Robert J. Bursik Jr. and Harold G. Grasmick** – highlighted the importance of strong social ties and a shared willingness among community members to intervene in crime prevention. More effective neighbourhoods tend to have lower crime rates.

CRIMINOLOGY TODAY AND TOMORROW

In 1970, legal scholar Lord Chorley described criminology as "the Cinderella of the social sciences". Like the fairytale character, criminology was initially overlooked and received far less attention, recognition and funding compared with its counterparts. Other social sciences, such as sociology, psychology and economics, had longer histories and track records of theoretical exploration. Criminology was often viewed as more concerned with *practical* solutions to crime, complicated by data collection methods and analysis.

For much of the twentieth century, criminology struggled to gain respect and acknowledgement as a legitimate and valuable field of study within academia and society. However, the twenty-first century hailed a new era for the discipline, where criminology's importance became widely recognized for understanding and addressing complex social issues related to crime, justice and public policy. This chapter introduces some of the topics that criminologists are engaged with today and the various debates that are expected to arise in the future. You will see how criminology continues to evolve as a respected and influential field within social sciences.

Who commits crime?

Understanding who commits crime is a central question in twenty-first century criminology. Differences in education levels or socioeconomic backgrounds between criminals and non-criminals can be relatively straightforward to measure, but more criminologists are also studying personality traits and preferences – which is much more difficult to assess. An international study published in 2022 showed that preferences such as risk tolerance, impatience, altruism and self-control can predict who will commit crime. In particular:

- Risk-tolerant, impatient young men are more likely to commit property crime.

- Low self-control strongly predicts violent, drug and sexual offences.

- Self-control significantly predicts crimes of passion but not property crime.

These findings are highly important. As one of the study's co-authors, Ernst Fehr, wrote: "The role that risk tolerance and patience play when it comes to crime propensity needs to be taken into account for crime prevention strategies."

Neurocriminology

Neurocriminology is a sub-discipline of criminology involving the integration of neuroscience, biology and criminology. It examines the genetic make-up and brain development of people involved in violence and other crimes to try to understand the "criminal mind". The central question that neurocriminology poses is: to what extent is an individual responsible for their actions? As criminologist Adrian Raine put it, if a criminal's brain functioning is impaired, then "how in the name of justice can we really hold that individual as responsible as we do?"

REDUCED PUNISHMENT

Biological and neurological explanations for criminal behaviour raise questions about the extent of responsibility and free will an individual has when committing a criminal offence, and therefore whether criminal punishments must change. For instance, an Italian court in 2009 reduced Abdelmalek Bayout's sentence for murder because neuroscientists found abnormalities in his brain scans and five genes linked to violent behaviour.

PHINEAS GAGE

The first case to suggest the brain's role in determining personality occurred in 1848. Gage, an American railroad worker, was involved in an accident in which a large iron rod was driven completely through his head (penetrating his left prefrontal cortex). Overnight, he turned from a kind and reliable man to a disinhibited and "uncontrollable" individual. Research has since shown prefrontal cortex damage is linked to antisocial behaviour and impaired impulse control.

Is crime in the genes?

A debate has always existed within criminology about whether genetic make-up determines our chances of engaging in criminal activity (see page 52). Today, criminologists are particularly interested in two types of genes:

- **Genes that control dopamine** – dopamine is a neurotransmitter, which acts as a chemical messenger in the brain. Variants in genes that control dopamine levels can lead to serious and violent antisocial behaviour.

- **Genes that control serotonin** – serotonin is a chemical that sends signals between nerve cells. Research shows low levels of serotonin are associated with increases in antisocial behaviour. A study in Pakistan led by scientist Muhammad Imran Qadeer showed genes that are important regulators of serotonin were major genetic determinants for criminal aggression.

Criminologists are exploring the possible consequences of genetic tests for criminal cases and assessing guilt. They are also questioning if genetic tests should be used to identify and treat personality disorders that are risk factors for criminal behaviour (thereby preventing future crime).

Social risk factors

Every society gets the kind of criminal it deserves.
What is equally true is that every community gets
the kind of law enforcement it insists on.
Robert F. Kennedy, American politician

An enduring question in criminology is why some areas have higher levels of crime. Research into social risk factors can help with answers, such as poverty, parental neglect, low self-esteem, alcohol and drug abuse, economics, and the wider community. Epidemiologist Anthony Fabio found that violence among boys was higher in disadvantaged neighbourhoods compared with their peers in more advantaged areas.

Criminologists want to address issues of racial inequality within the justice system. A 2023 study led by academic Ayobami Laniyonu looked at how racial disparity data collected by police are often inaccurate because they rely on officer perception of a stopped person's race, which can be inconsistent with how individuals self-identify. Research can assist law enforcement officers to address unconscious bias and create policies to reduce racial disparities in sentencing and the use of force.

Family-based risks

Criminologists generally agree that adverse family circumstances increase the risk of delinquent behaviour, especially a lack of parental oversight, poor attachment, divorce/separation and frequent switching in caregivers. For instance:

- **Lack of structure** – studies show that teenagers from families characterized by a lack of order and discipline are four times more at risk of engaging in delinquent behaviour as adults than children from structured families.

- **Fatherless homes** – in the US, research shows that 90 per cent of people who commit serious crimes have absent fathers. People with absent fathers also make up 75 per cent of adolescent murderers and 70 per cent of juveniles in prison. Eighty per cent of the population of rapists with diagnosed anger problems also come from fatherless homes.

- **Poor attachment** – a 2012 meta-analysis of delinquency studies found poor attachment to parents was significantly linked to delinquency in boys and girls, and that the benefits of strong attachment were strongest if the child and the parent had the same sex (so boys benefit from a strong attachment to their father, and girls benefit from a strong attachment to their mother).

Criminologists continue to use studies such as these to identify vulnerable young people and design interventions that focus on these critical relationships.

ABSENCE AT THE CELLULAR LEVEL

In 2017, scientists found a measurable biological outcome related to the absence of a father, especially before the age of nine. They saw a significant adverse effect on telomeres (sequences of DNA found at the ends of chromosomes) – a core biological indicator of health. The findings suggest that public policy should strive to maintain contact between children and fathers, such as alternative punishments in the event of incarceration.

Mental health and trauma

In 2023, the World Health Organization reported that one-third of the prison population in Europe suffered from mental health disorders. Likewise, a study in 2017 found that one-third of all inmates in the US were diagnosed with a mental disorder prior to their imprisonment. Researchers are therefore questioning which factors can increase or decrease the risk of criminal behaviour for the small minority of individuals with mental health conditions who commit crimes.

Links between childhood trauma and crime are also being explored. A study in 2022 showed that people who have suffered extreme difficulties in childhood (such as poverty, maltreatment or school exclusion) are more likely to commit crimes as adults than those who have not. Professor Susan McVie suggested that policy changes are needed across different sectors if crime is to be prevented, including "increasing educational attainment, reducing child poverty, improving adolescent health and well-being, and dealing effectively with child maltreatment".

The economist Elisa Jácome has recommended improved access to mental health care as an effective way to reduce crime, because "those with better mental health are more likely to understand – and be deterred by – the consequences of criminal activity."

UNSAFE NEIGHBOURHOODS

Criminologists are addressing crime and mental health from a variety of angles, including the impact of unsafe neighbourhoods on the mental health of residents (including those who are not direct victims of crime). Studies show that people living in unsafe areas are more likely to report mental health problems, including depression, anxiety and psychological distress.

Poor diet

One of the most profound influences on criminal behaviour is surprisingly mundane – food and nutrition. In 2014, research scientist Bernard Gesch studied how the addition of previously missing nutrients to the diets of young adult prisoners (18–21 years) affected their behaviour. Those taking supplements for at least two weeks committed 37 per cent fewer serious offences, including violence. Gesch believes nutritious food or supplements could provide "a simple and humane means to help reduce and prevent a significant proportion of violence and antisocial behaviour". Unlike other initiatives to reduce crime, improving nutrition is relatively cheap and shows quick results.

ALCOHOL

Alcohol consumption is also a major contributor to crime in many countries. In the UK, alcohol fuels almost 40 per cent of violent crimes and half of domestic violence. In the US, a study found 86 per cent of homicide offenders and 60 per cent of sexual offenders had used alcohol before or during the crime.

Hormones

A growing body of research is investigating how hormones like testosterone and cortisol can affect criminal behaviour. For example, higher levels of testosterone have been linked to increased aggression and dominance, potentially contributing to violent crimes. Elevated cortisol levels in response to chronic stress can lead to impaired decision-making and emotional regulation.

Liars have been found to experience a bigger spike in cortisol compared with those who tell the truth, especially when discussing something they did wrong. As psychologist Robert Josephs summarized: "Elevated testosterone decreases the fear of punishment while increasing sensitivity to reward... Testosterone furnishes the courage to cheat, and elevated cortisol provides a reason to cheat."

THE PREMENSTRUAL DEFENDANT

In 1981, two British women escaped murder convictions by arguing that their legal responsibility was diminished by premenstrual syndrome (PMS). Criminologists are studying whether women who commit crimes while experiencing PMS or premenstrual dysphoric disorder (PMDD) should be held fully responsible for their actions.

Unhealthy gangs

*The gang is life, often rough and untamed, yet
rich in elemental social processes significant to
the student of society and human nature.*
Frederic Thrasher, sociologist

Criminal gangs pose a safety threat across societies
worldwide, and studies show that they are among the
most violent of all criminal offenders. For over a century,
criminologists have conducted a huge amount of research
into the way gangs emerge and evolve, why people
join gangs, and the urban and political conditions that
encourage their formation.

Today, more criminologists are exploring health
problems associated with gang membership. Various
studies show that gang members are significantly more
likely to experience heart trouble, kidney problems and
hypertension, as well as psychological distress, such as
depression and anxiety. They are also at high risk of being
victims of physical violence. A study by psychologists Jane
Wood and Sophie Dennard found street gang prisoners
had more symptoms of paranoia and post-traumatic stress
disorder compared with non-gang prisoners.

Pollution and hot temperatures

The connection between pollution and crime is becoming a critical issue. Researchers have found that air pollution is a major factor of crime in London, especially shoplifting and pickpocketing. A study found the crime rate in London was 8.4 per cent higher on the most polluted day compared with the least polluted day. It is believed that poor air quality may cause spikes in cortisol (see page 125). This suggests that improving air quality could reduce minor crimes.

Climate has also been associated with increased levels of violence. Almost 8,000 shootings in US cities between 2015–2020 were thought to be influenced by unseasonably warm temperatures. Researchers believe the reason lies in your body heating up, causing an elevated blood pressure and heart rate. The discomfort from these physical reactions triggers anger and aggression in some individuals. As researcher Laurence Wainwright explained: "Even fairly small changes in temperature can have a connection with biological, psychological and social factors that influence the way humans behave, including their propensity for violence."

Urban design

The importance of access to safe public spaces has gradually been recognized. In 2017, it was made a global priority as a UN Sustainable Development Goal. However, stretched police forces often mean convictions for property and street crime are rare, as forces' attention is elsewhere or they lack the resources to conduct full and effective investigations. Criminologists are researching ways to increase the safety of public spaces through redesigning the layout and landscaping of urban areas. For instance:

- The regeneration of public spaces in deprived neighbourhoods significantly increases people's sense of safety.

- Pre-emptively identifying environmental weaknesses, like damaged CCTV, street lighting and alley gates.

- Increasing the public's use of social media community messaging systems to share pictures of suspicious vehicles or visitors to homes captured on doorbell cameras.

- Analyzing the use of social media, like police accounts on X (formerly Twitter), or Facebook and YouTube activity, to map and alert potentially dangerous zones of interaction.

FEMALE FEARS

Research shows men are more likely to be victims of crime, but women experience higher worry about crime, principally because of fear of sexual violence. Criminologists have identified "protective behavioural responses" often practised by women in urban spaces, such as restricting their destinations, routes, times and modes of transport, and increased confinement in the home.

As landscape planner Pablo Navarrete-Hernandez wrote in 2023, there are "profound gender gaps in the right to access and seize city opportunities", impacting women's employment, education and well-being. Feminist researchers argue that urban planners and designers often fail to consider women's legitimate safety concerns.

Looking at social harms

It is not simply that a focus on crime deflects attention from other more socially pressing harms; in many respects it positively excludes them.
Paddy Hillyard and Steve Tombs, academics

Criminologists are increasingly shifting the focus of their work away from crime to "social harms", including economic, physical, psychological and emotional harms. This approach (also known as zemiology) is based on the idea that any activity, process or set of circumstances that is harmful or damaging is worthy of attention, regardless of whether it is against the law.

Rather than the narrow and individualistic approach of criminal responsibility, it allows a wider investigation into causes and accountability. It is especially helpful for harms that go beyond national boundaries, such as damage to the environment. The actions of nation states often affect people and places outside their territory. State harm, environmental offences, corporate offences and workplace injury are just some of the areas being explored.

Green criminology

Criminologist Michael J. Lynch introduced the term "green criminology" to describe the study of crimes against the environment, animals and nature, and the social and economic factors contributing to these offences. This subfield of criminology has grown significantly, and Australian criminologist Rob White has identified three broad categories:

- **Environmental Justice** – how environmental harm disproportionately affects marginalized communities, highlighting social inequalities related to ecological destruction.

- **Ecological Justice** – the harm inflicted upon ecosystems and non-human species, emphasizing protecting the environment and biodiversity from human-induced damage.

- **Species Justice** – the ethical treatment of animals and advocating for their rights against animal cruelty, poaching and exploitation.

Research is expanding into areas that were previously neglected, such as agricultural practices, the victimization of indigenous people, children's exposure to toxic chemicals and electronic waste, and animal labour.

Alternatives to prison

The degree of civilization in a society can be judged by entering its prisons.
Fyodor Dostoevsky, Russian author

The US has over 20 per cent of the world's total prison population. The year 2023 marked the fiftieth year since the US prison population began an unprecedented surge, from 200,000 in 1974 to over 2 million by 2023, with Black Americans being vastly overrepresented. However, the increased rates of incarceration had no demonstrated effect on violent crime. Criminologists are continuously researching alternatives, especially:

- **Restorative Justice** – focuses on the rehabilitation of offenders by bringing them together with victims and their wider community. In some cases, victims confront their attackers, seek financial restitution or have a say on the programmes the offender must undertake.

- **Rehabilitation** – helping offenders address the root causes of their behaviour, such as substance abuse, mental health problems and trauma. Research shows it is effective at reducing repeat offending and promoting public safety. It can include cognitive behavioural therapy, addiction treatment or vocational training to help offenders develop the skills they need to succeed in society.

While prison can be a default solution for many crimes, criminological research exposes its possible dangers and allows us to see other ways to improve public safety.

TIME INSIDE

Inmates at the Sant'Angelo dei Lombardi prison in Italy work on the site in paid jobs including wine making, farming or dry cleaning. The best-behaved have their own separate kitchen and can make themselves pasta. Halden, an "open prison" in Norway, has no barred windows or security cameras, and guards are unarmed, despite the site holding prisoners like murderers and rapists.

Policing

Across the globe, law enforcement has been rapidly changing during the twenty-first century. With new forms of crime and technological advancements, as well as spending restrictions and shifts in society, criminologists are exploring options for new policing strategies and tools. By exploring how criminal behaviour might change over the coming years and the challenges that lie ahead – such as rising inequality or climate change – criminologists can identify what action should be taken to prepare current and future officers.

A TECHNOLOGICAL ARMS RACE

Criminals often use the latest technology to commit their offences, forcing police to quickly adopt the same innovations. In 1912, the Bonnot Gang robbed a bank outside Paris and escaped in an automobile – they were pursued by two police officers: one riding a bicycle and the other on horseback! In the 2020s, cyber laundering required law enforcement departments worldwide to develop new methods for tracking financial activity.

Crime-fighting technology

Artificial intelligence (AI), automation, big data and extended reality are transforming life today. Criminologists use these technological developments to access a wealth of knowledge regarding human behaviour and hidden patterns in different situations. In 2010, the Los Angeles Police Department developed a mathematical model using crime data to create an algorithm that spots crime patterns – many police departments around the world replicated it.

Lior Rokach, head of Israel's Center for Computational Criminology, said in 2018: "The AI revolution of the past few years will prove to be even more significant than DNA testing for law enforcement, providing them with unprecedented investigative tools and new sources of evidence." Predictive policing tools used in the British city of Manchester were responsible for reductions of 12 per cent in robberies, 21 per cent in burglaries and 32 per cent in vehicle theft. These developments come with risks (see page 138), so criminologists are studying the regulation of surveillance and AI technologies, the benefits of ethical supervision boards, continuous algorithmic revision and privacy protection laws.

Crime data analysis

Technological developments in the twenty-first century have revolutionized the way law enforcement agencies work to prevent, investigate and analyze crimes. Crime data analysis has benefited from new digital tools. Here are some of the methods used for identifying patterns and trends in criminal activity:

- Drones are used as eyes in the sky; they allow officers to observe areas and capture screenshots and videos as digital evidence.

- Data mapping provides a clear geographical view of crimes, their types and frequency, allowing law enforcement officers to track common crimes and develop crime prevention strategies.

- Global positioning systems (GPS) allows offenders and police officers to be tracked easily and quickly.

- Social network analysis techniques have been widely employed to detect criminal networks.

Criminologists are exploring how these technologies can allow law enforcement to be less reactive and more proactive.

Blockchain technology

Blockchains are digital ledgers or databases that track transactions across numerous computers in a secure and decentralized way. They make data **immutable** – meaning tamper-proof and irreversible. Though blockchain technology has mostly been used for cryptocurrencies, criminologists have recognized its possible use in the criminal justice system. It could enhance the security of sensitive documents, speed up pretrial operations, improve document storage and even expose false evidence.

Maintaining accurate, up-to-date criminal histories has historically required vast amounts of manual data entry, ongoing audits and quality-control procedures. Blockchain could be used from the moment a suspect is arrested, while prosecutors, courts and criminal-history repositories would instantly be updated.

TRACKING CONVICTS

Since 2018, convicts on parole in some Chinese cities have been tracked over a blockchain network. When prisoners are released, they're required to wear electronic bracelets fitted with a tracking encryption so that they can be tracked in real time and their employment efforts monitored.

Artificial intelligence

AI presents a new era for crime prediction and prevention. AI facial recognition skills are improving crowd surveillance results by establishing the identity and location of suspects. AI can assess clothing, skeletal structure and body movements to detect abnormal or suspicious behaviour in large crowds, allowing for the early detection of shoplifters or dangerous drivers. Beyond its potential to enhance public safety, criminologists are also exploring the risks:

DISCRIMINATION

The potential for bias in AI algorithms can lead to unfair targeting of certain groups. Evidence shows that human prejudices have been baked into these tools because the machine-learning models are trained on biased police data. In 2016, Chinese researchers Xiaolin Wu and Xi Zhang reported that they could apply their computer algorithm to scanned facial photos and predict with 89.5 per cent accuracy whether a person is a criminal. Their algorithm identified "some discriminating structural features for predicting criminality, such as lip curvature, eye inner corner distance, and the so-called nose–mouth angle".

PRIVACY

The use of AI often involves the collection and analysis of personal data, such as photos from social media (without users' consent).

LACK OF TRANSPARENCY

It can be hard to understand how a machine-learning algorithm arrived at a particular decision, which makes it difficult to identify and correct errors or biases.

PREDICTIVE POLICING

Officers expect trouble when on patrol, making them more likely to stop or arrest people because of prejudice rather than need. The accumulated arrests skew the system to send even more police to the area, which deprives other areas of policing.

Research by criminologists is a vital part of the effort to ensure that AI is used in an ethical and just way.

Conclusion

In 2014, the distinguished British criminologist David Faulkner wrote: "People should be thought of and respected as people, not treated as an assembly of 'needs' and 'risks' which have to be 'addressed' as if the person were a machine to be serviced." This poignant statement encapsulates the essence of criminology. It dares to challenge media portrayals, public perceptions of criminals and our own prejudices.

From theories that probe the deepest recesses of the human psyche to the examination of institutions that shape societal responses, criminologists reveal the web of factors that drive individuals to break the law. By investigating the root causes of criminal behaviour, the dynamics of criminal justice and the impact of policy choices, criminology is a powerful tool for effecting change. Its research informs psychology, sociology, law through which to view countless other fields, offering a unique lens at crime and its consequences. Criminological studies expose whether our criminal justice practices truly reflect the values we claim to uphold and, ultimately, move us closer to a stronger society.

Further Reading

Angela Kirwin, *Criminal: How Our Prisons Are Failing Us All* (2022)

Baz Dreisinger, *Incarceration Nations: A Journey to Justice in Prisons Around the World* (2016)

Brandon L. Garrett, *Convicting the Innocent: Where Criminal Prosecutions Go Wrong* (2011)

Craig Haney, *Criminality in Context: The Psychological Foundations of Criminal Justice Reform* (2020)

David Grann, *Killers of the Flower Moon: The Osage Murders and the Birth of the FBI* (2017)

Geoffrey Wansell, *Lifers: Inside the Minds of Britain's Most Notorious Criminals* (2016)

Gwen Adshead and Eileen Horne, *The Devil You Know: Encounters in Forensic Psychiatry* (2022)

Jennifer Thompson-Cannino Jennifer and Ronald Cotton, *Picking Cotton: Our Memoir of Injustice and Redemption* (2009)

Miles Johnson, *Chasing Shadows: A True Story of Drugs, War and the Secret World of International Crime* (2023)

**THE LITTLE
BOOK OF
ANTHROPOLOGY**

Rasha Barrage

Paperback

978-1-80007-415-6

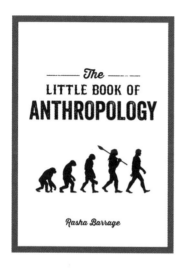

This illuminating little book will introduce you to the key thinkers, themes and theories you need to know to understand the development of human beings, and how our history has informed the way we live today. A perfect gift for anyone taking their first steps into the world of anthropology, as well as for those who want to brush up their knowledge.

**THE LITTLE
BOOK OF
SOCIOLOGY**

Rasha Barrage

Paperback

978-1-80007-718-8

If you've always wanted to know how societies function – and why sometimes they don't – this beginner's guide to sociology has got the essential theories and thinkers covered.

Sociology has almost limitless scope. From the smallest everyday interaction to the impact of vast systemic change, societies are brimming with fascinating phenomena we all want to understand more clearly.

Have you enjoyed this book? If so, find us on
Facebook at **Summersdale Publishers**, on Twitter/X
at **@Summersdale** and on Instagram and TikTok at
@summersdalebooks and get in touch.
We'd love to hear from you!

www.summersdale.com

IMAGE CREDITS
Cover image and throughout – fingerprint
© Alex109/Shutterstock.com